NO RETURN

A Real, Live Look At
RUTH

BRING 'EM BACK
ALIVE!
character study series

D1529761

C. Celeste Palmer

Cook Ministry Resources
a division of Cook Communications Ministries
Colorado Springs, Colorado/Paris, Ontario

BRING 'EM BACK ALIVE
No Return: A Real, Live Look at Ruth

Scripture quotations are from the Holy Bible, New International Version (NIV), © 1973, 1978, 1984 by the International Bible Society. Used by permission of Zondervan Bible Publishers.

Series creator: Randy Southern
Series editor: Rick Wesselhoff
Designer: Sonya Duckworth
Cover Illustrator: Gregory Dye
Interior Illustrator: Gregory Dye

Cook Ministry Resources
a division of Cook Communications Ministries
4050 Lee Vance View
Colorado Springs, CO 80918-7100
Cable address: DCCOOK

Printed in U. S. A.

ISBN: 0-7814-5238-4

Table of Contents

Introduction to Bring 'Em Back Alive 4

session one: **Good Grief**
The heart-breaking story of three widows left with nothing 5

session two: **Forever Friends**
How a true friendship grew in the most unlikely of places 15

session three: **When Life Takes You to the Gleaners**
The story of God's welfare reform program 23

session four: **Playing the Field**
Romance heats up between Bo and Ruth 31

session five: **It's All in the G.E.N.E.S.**
A changed identity; a shocker of an ending 41

INTRODUCTION TO
Bring 'Em Back Alive

The stakes are high.

Depression. Loneliness. Parents getting divorced. AIDS. Suicide. Gangs. Drugs. "If you really loved me, you'd go all the way." The New Age. Bitterness. . . No one has to tell you: The stakes are high.

In the next five weeks, a lot can happen in your students' lives. A lot *will* happen. You can't afford to simply "play church." You need a curriculum that understands where your teens live.

Maybe that's why you've chosen *Bring 'Em Back Alive.*
• Because the new generation of youth can't relate to doctored-up, picture-perfect portraits of biblical "superheros." *Bring 'Em Back Alive* is REAL.
• Because your teens don't want to be told what to think. They learn from relationships. *Bring 'Em Back Alive* is about people. Not memory verses. It tells by story. Not by preaching.
• Because you face a stiff challenge trying to bring biblical truth to MTV kids. *Bring 'Em Back Alive* is the total package. Interactive learning. Discussion starters. Extra action options. Biblical depth.

NO RETURN, one in the series of *Bring 'Em Back Alive,* was written with one thought in mind: to challenge your teens to take their faith past the point of No Return. Ruth's story speaks for itself. It's the story of a life-crushed widow struggling to hang on to her humanity in a world that forgot about her. It's the story of how God comes through when there's finally no where else to turn. The bold moves Ruth takes will challenge your students. What she finds on the other side of faith will encourage them.

But don't think that means five long weeks until we get there. Along the way, Ruth will find a coping strategy that works, deal with being labeled, face sexual temptation, and assume a new identity.

One final note: We've packed this character study series chock full of extra ideas, tips, tidbits, options, and background information. Use what works for you. Here's a guide to help you know what to expect when you see the following icons:

 To help you connect the main character to other people and events from Scripture, we've included the *Biblical Rewind* and *Biblical Fast Forward* side bars.

 On the first page of every session you'll find the lesson "in a nutshell." The *Profile* paragraph summarizes what happens to the main character.

 Interject some action. Go a different direction. Add an activity. The *Optional Extra* side bars let you customize the lesson to your group.

 The *Key Point* paragraph tells you up front where the lesson's going. This is also on the first page of each session.

The *Info Byte* side bars will put you in touch with the facts, background, and research you need to teach the text.

session one:

Good Grief

[handwritten note, right margin]: Right before step 3 start by reading Ruth 1:11-18 through have them jot down words or thoughts that jump out to them. Prayer for understanding

PROFILE

Soon after moving his family from the small Jewish town of Bethlehem to Moab, Elimelech died. Ignoring the intense, bitter feud between the Jews and the Moabites, Naomi allowed her sons to marry Moabite women. But some ten years later, tragedy struck again. Both sons died. Now, there were three helpless, hopeless widows—Naomi and her daughters-in-law, Ruth and Orpah. Long before the days of prenuptial agreements, Moabite law left no inheritance rights to the wives. No camel convertible. No house on Eucalyptus and Sycamore. That's what you call a Massive Bummer. Left without many good options, Naomi ambled back to Bethlehem. Orpah stayed in Moab. And Ruth was forced to choose between a rock and a hard place: return to her empty life in Moab or follow Naomi into Israel. For some reason, Ruth insisted on accompanying her bitter, depressed, penniless mother-in-law into a strange land where people vehemently despised Moabites. Go figure! She walked right past the point of No Return and never looked back on her old way of life. Her bold move of faith has a lot to say to us about how to deal with our own tough spots.

KEY POINT

Tough times require bold faith. Lean hard.
Life is tough. God won't shelter us from that. He's more interested in how we choose to deal with disaster: Do we learn to lean on Him for better or worse, or do we turn around and head back to where we started? As for you, milk your faith for all it's worth. Pass the point of No Return.

step **1**	step **4**

step **1**
- Extra-large, black leaf bags or other garbage bags
- Stash of old magazines and newspapers
- Scissors, tape, streamers, buttons, other creative materials
- Prize
- *Variation*: posterboard, creative supplies

step **2**
- Trash can or mini-coffin

step **4**
- Copies of Resource 1
- Eraserboard or newsprint, marker
- *Optional Extra*: TV, VCR, pre-recorded clips from TV shows on videocassette tape
- *Optional Extra*: bitter foods, sweet foods
- Pens and paper
- *Optional Extra*: blindfolds

step **5**
- *Variation*: index cards and pens
- Copies of Resource 2, scissors, tape
- *Optional Extra*: CD player, copy of the song "Ironic" on CD

step 1 GARBAGE GARB

Students make "Garbage Garb" by decorating bags with personal symbols.
Pass out one garbage bag per student and have teens make "Garbage Garbs" by ripping out holes for their heads and arms. Let them have at a pile of magazines you bring in to clip headlines, pictures, and words that represent all that they own and all that is important to them. Students should then tape these pictures, along with other odds and ends, to their bags. Encourage wild, wacky creativity; for example, streamers could represent partying with friends, or a dollar bill could represent their all-important cash stash. Do one yourself! Give prizes for the most creative outfit. See how many include God in some way on their Garbage Garb. Compare outfits, and rant and rave about the creativity of your students.

[**VARIATION**: Paste the pictures and objects to posterboard. Wherever "Garbage Garb" is referred to below, substitute your "Clippings Creations."]

step 2 TRASHED!

Students trash all the items on their garb and discuss what it's like to lose everything.
Sit in a large circle around a trash can. (For extra effect, bring in a mini-coffin, available in some novelty stores.) Say: **Now strip off your garbage garb the one thing that means the most to you.** This is a great chance to get students to share what matters most in their life. **Slam dunk that item into the trash can. Imagine that this thing has just been stripped out of your life.** Discuss one or both of the following questions:

- **Have you ever experienced the loss of someone or something important to you? How did it feel?**
- **If this was for real and you lost the thing most important to you, what would you do? Would you get angry and punch something? Would you go up to your room and talk to nobody? Or what?**

Have students imagine that *everything* important in their life is stripped away. Slam dunk all Garbage Garb items into the trash. (See Optional Extra.)

Read the following paragraph, leaving a couple silent seconds after each question: **Now you're a bunch of bag ladies and bag guys. (Get it? Bag**

ladies, like garbage bags.) You have nothing left in your life. You don't have any family to come home to. You've lost the people you've loved the most. You have no place to go. You own almost nothing. What are you going to do about all this? How do you feel inside? Angry? Sad? Depressed? How do you feel towards God?

Now, I want you to make a mental note right now of how this feels. Today, we're going to learn about a trio of women who lost everything.

journal bit

Step 3 TRAGEDY STRIKES

Students read and discuss the three widows' tragedy in Ruth 1:1-7.

Before diving in to the passage, you may want to give some background on the time period of the Judges. (See Biblical Rewind.) Read Ruth 1:1-2. Ask: **What's the deal here? Did Elimelilaliac or whatever his name is . . . Did this E-Mel guy have a persecution complex? Why would anybody want to live in enemy territory with no rights and constant put-downs?** Take a few guesses as to why he made the move. Maybe he was bored with all God's rules, or maybe he knew he was dying and wanted to be a world-traveler. But if no one gets it, point out that famine has a funny way of making people do desperate things.

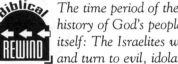
The time period of the Judges is a blotched spot in the history of God's people. A disturbing cycle repeated itself: The Israelites would forget their Lord Yahweh and turn to evil, idolatry, and perversion. Yahweh would send a nation to oppress them until they cried out to God again for help. Yahweh would then raise up a spiritual and military leader—a Judge—who would lead Israel back to worship of God. Once again, life was good. That is, until Israel forgot Yahweh and repeated the cycle all over again.

Pick three volunteers. Have one represent Elimelech and the other two Moabites. Say: **Moabites hated the Israelites. When E-Mel came to town, there was sure to be some prejudice. E-Mel was sure to be pushed around a bit.** Have the Moabite volunteers yell and push around the Elimelech character.

Explain that after her husband kicks the bucket, Naomi's next move is also lifted from the "What were they thinking?" files. The long-standing feud between Moab and Israel was so bad that God had banned Moabites from the congregation of the Lord until the tenth generation. (See Info Byte.) Scripture commanded the Israelites to do no more than show a cold shoulder to the Moabites. But Naomi allowed her two sons to marry foreigners. **What was Naomi thinking?** Take a few guesses: Maybe she couldn't take it being a foreigner anymore. Maybe at her husband's death, she lost her faith in God. Or maybe the girls were incredibly rich and had a widowed father that Naomi had the hots for. Either way, be sure to point out that intermarriage with the Moabites was against the better judgment of most Israelites.

Here's the facts: E-Mel moves to a God-forsaken country and croaks shortly after. His two sons take a couple of apparently God-rejected Moabite girls for wives, and before you know it, the sons are pushing up daisies, too. That's three bad choices. Three tragic deaths. Is this God's idea of punishment? We know this is a Youth Worker's Nightmare Question. We know this will open a can of worms, as in: Why does a loving God allow people to suffer? But, stick with us. Your students' opinions and questions here will create a focus for the rest of the session.

Moab was the country founded by the descendants of Lot from an incestuous relationship with his daughters. (See Gen. 19:30-38.) When the Israelites fled the Egyptians, the Moabites refused to give them food, water, or passage through their land. They even killed off and raided the stragglers in the exile group, causing more hostility. God banned Moabites from the congregation of the Lord "until the tenth generation" (Deut. 23:3), which some commentators think was a figurative way to say forever. This story is written in a time of relative military calm between the two nations; but the anger, prejudice, and hatred between them was as fresh as ever.

Read Ruth 1:6, 7. **Just when you thought things couldn't get any worse . . .** *Road Trip With The Mother In Law!* **Imagine: day after day of of walking in the blistering, unmerciful desert sun. You're convinced your legs are about to fall off. And the worst part about it is, you're stuck listening to your whiney, complaining, bitter mother-in-law! You can bet that trip was a real soul-searching time for everybody involved. How each of those women decided to handle the crisis they were in would shape the rest of their lives.**

step 4 TEEN HELP HOT-LINE

Students role-play peer counselors and advise the three widows in their grief.
You all are volunteers at the Teen Peer Counseling Hot-Line. It's a busy night on the phones tonight, so some of you are going to get your chance to counsel teens that are dealing with loneliness, grief, and even depression. Have students break into teams of six or less. (If it's less, some students will have to play two different roles.) Pass out copies of Resource 1, "Hot-Line Help." In each group assign the following roles: Ruth, Orpah, Naomi, and three peer counselors. Using the cards that correspond with their characters or using their best judgement as peer counselors, have students take turns role-playing what a conversation might have sounded like if Naomi, Ruth and Orpah had called in to the hot-line.

Allow ample time for students to grapple with what kind of advice they would give. Then come back together in a large group and discuss what students learned. Ask: **On your team, who gave the best advice? What was it?** Let a spokesperson from each team respond briefly.

[VARIATION: If you have a small group, you may want to assign three volunteers to the characters Ruth, Naomi, and Orpah. Then have them stand in front of the class and role-play their call into the Teen Help Hot-Line. All of your other students can take turns offering their best advice by raising their hands and waiting to be called on by you.]

The rest of Step 4 is broken into three subsections dealing with the three different ways Ruth, Naomi and Orpah dealt with The Crisis. Read through Ruth 1:8-22 to get an overview of the Bible-base from which the above character sketches came from. (See Info Byte.) Tell students to pay special attention to the decision Orpah made in verse 14. Ask:

- **Each one caller had a different way of handling their loss and loneliness. How did Orpah handle it? Was this a good move or bad?**
- **Based on this action, how much of a priority do you think her relationship with God was to her?**

On eraserboard or newsprint, write "BEATEN DOWN."

Add the following info as needed: Students should be able to identify that Orpah did what would have been considered normal or natural in her situation. She went back to her old family and friends. And her old god. Explain that at one point, Orpah may have come close to a belief in the God of Israel. After all, she did begin the long trek to Israel and what was there for her, except maybe faith in a god who didn't kill babies? (See Info Byte.)

In ancient times when a husband died, all of his property and belongings went to the man who owned the family birthright. Widows were left with absolutely nothing. Israelite law provided that if a widow had sons, they were to provide for her. But Naomi, Ruth and Orpah had no sons. If no one would take care of the widow, she would spend the rest of her life in dire poverty while often being taken advantage of by many men. If a widow had no sons, she could return to her family as Orpah did. If her husband had brothers, they were to marry her and provide for her, but neither Naomi's nor Ruth's husband apparently had living brothers. Their plight was severe indeed.

Moabites worshiped an idol god named Chemosh, who demanded annual child sacrifice.

Wherever she was on her faith journey, Orpah tubed any potential she had to get to know God. With one decision, she lost out on learning about The Ultimate Relationship. In essence, she chose the easy route. Instead of learning from her crisis, she chose to go right back to all the things she was familiar and secure with. (At least she'd have a chance of landing a husband.) While it's a good coping strategy to surround yourself with a support system, in a sense Orpah was Beaten Down by her grief. She ended up right back where she started. Same old painful life. She learned nothing. Most importantly, she missed out on knowing the true God. (See Optional Extra.)

Have students turn to the person next to them and quickly share some of the favorite coping mechanisms they use when life gets tough. Student responses might include: oversleep, overeat, dump on friends, lock myself in the bathroom for forty days, veg in front of the TV, pray, get high, etc. No matter what their habit of choice might be, challenge students to file away this question for times of pain and grief: **God, what are you trying to say to me through this tough time?** Affirm that no matter how deep the mess gets in their life, this question can often lead down surprising paths.

Rescan the passage again, this time paying special attention to Naomi's attitude in Ruth 1:11-13.

- **How did Naomi handle her grief? Would you say this is a good coping strategy or not?**
- **What does this show about her relationship with God?**

On eraserboard or newsprint write "BITTER."

Add the following info as needed: Students should be able to identify that Naomi believed she was being punished and afflicted by God. She didn't totally tube her relationship with God, but she let it turn bitter. In the depths of despair, she saw God as the cause of everything bad that happened. She felt forsaken by God. Sometimes bitterness is the only response we know how to give to massive tragedy. It's our *real* response. And God understands that. He does not move away and He will not abandon His people. But students have to understand that when they *hang out* in the house of bitterness, it's one of the most destructive choices they can make. Naomi's fault wasn't in seeing God's sovereignty over all things. God *is* sovereign. God *is* in control. Her fault was in not seeing the *goodness* in His sovereignty; namely, that even in the midst of trial God was still present, still good, and still offering support and not condemnation. Encourage students to work through their own bitter feelings. Naomi says that God brought her back to Israel empty. But the truth is, He desperately wanted to refill her with stuff better than what was in her to start with! (See Optional Extra.)

Either silently or on paper, have students identify one specific area in which they might have bitterness in their hearts. Challenge them to take this one-on-one with God. Has an unanswered prayer caused unresolved emotions? Have they struggled to make sense of some severe tragedy? Give students time to silently bring their concerns into the presence of God. Encourage them to be brutally honest about what might be troubling their hearts. Remind students that God is big enough to handle our anger. He stands right by us wanting to help us work through our emotions.

Make a videotape of clips of TV characters coping with crises. Get a good mix, from the dysfunctional habits of The Simpsons, to the real-life struggles to hold on to humanity found in shows like High Incident and E.R. If you don't watch a lot of TV, you might delegate this assignment to a few of your students. Watch the clips during the session. After each clip, discuss the pros and cons of the coping mechanism. Discuss: **What does the rest of the world usually think of "leaning on God" as a coping mechanism? How do you think it stacks up to some of the more popular coping mechanisms?**

Bring in a couple of bitter foods and set these on a table—a radish, a turnip, horseradish sauce for dip, etc. Also bring in some sweet foods—cookies, ice cream, etc. Call on a couple of volunteers and give them the choice of tasting the bitter foods or the sweet foods. Give a huge sales pitch for the bitter foods. Regardless, most of your volunteers will quickly hone in on the sweets. Discuss: **How does this example about food relate to our emotional lives? Is it true that we all would rather taste the sweet side of life than the bitter side? Then why do some people stay bitter? Bitterness is a place we all end up at sometimes, but do you know of people who want to stay there? Who likes to continue to stay angry without healing or to complain without moving towards resolution?**

OPTIONAL **TAKE ONE** *EXTRA*

Use eye patches or strips of cloth to blindfold your students over one eye. If you and your students are comfortable with this, tell them to pair off and rotate giving each other back rubs. Have a student you've prepared ahead of time interrupt and say: **You guys, you all can only see with one eye! Take a risk; come follow me and I'll teach you to see what you've been missing.** *Sit back and take note of who takes your volunteer up on the risk. For those students that do, your volunteer should place a blindfold over both eyes and lead them around the room for a few minutes before lifting the blindfold off. Afterwards say:* **This is what it's like to pass the point of No Return in your walk with God. You're chillin' out. Everything's comfortable. And you don't even know that you're missing some good stuff in life. God says to you, "Take a risk and follow Me." But following Him means being blind for a while and not knowing where you're going. In a series of bold moves, Ruth made herself available to God. Once she passed the point of No Return in her faith, God pursued her and connected with her.**

Take a look at the passage again and pay special attention to Ruth's response in Ruth 1:16-18.

- **How did Ruth deal with her losses? How does this coping strategy stack against the others?**
- **What does this say about her faith in God?**

On eraserboard or newsprint, write "BELIEF."

Add the following info as needed: Students should be able to identify that Ruth had learned an important lesson in the middle of her tragedy. She found a comforting relationship with the God of the Universe. She could lose her husband, and all her "stuff." But if she gained a relationship with the Lord out of the deal, she still came out miles ahead. Ruth knew that the Lord would be there with her every step of the way. He is the Sovereign Comforter, not the Sovereign Punisher. Why an all-powerful, all-loving God allows tragedy to happen is one of the ultimate mysteries of this universe. But part of the answer comes in Romans 8:28 which says that God causes all things to work out for good in the end, for those who love Him. Although we can't understand all the reasons fully, one of the reasons God allows pain and suffering in the world is to put the ball in our court. Will we learn to trust God with our hurts and pains, or will we go through life thinking we can do it on our own? When the ball was in her court, Ruth stepped up, put her faith on the line, and passed the point of No Return. (See Optional Extra.)

Hand out paper and pencils. Have students write down a couple of the major setbacks or big-time struggles they currently face or have faced from the archives of their past. They can write initials or a code name if they're worried about others around them seeing something personal. Have them write down "bitter"; "beaten down"; or, "belief" next to each struggle indicating which phrase comes closest to describing their response to that situation. Share from your own life a time when you suffered a serious loss. You don't necessarily have to make yourself sound like a spiritual giant here. Be honest about a time when you were beaten down or bitter and talk about what consequences that had in your life. Also, tell how in looking back on God's grace you can see the specific ways He drew you into relationship and filled you up again. Make sure that students know you're not encouraging them to go out and be spiritually mature overnight, to be completely trusting of God in every great tragedy of their life starting now. Instead, focus on celebrating how good God is to us in the midst of trial no matter where we're at. For example, even though Naomi was bitter, God was still there for her. He unfolded great blessings for her throughout the story of Ruth.

[**VARIATION**: If you feel the need to make this step a little more personal, take turns sharing one recent crisis that each group member is facing. Ask:

- **Is there anything we can do as a group to support you?**
- **What do you need to move from being "beaten down" or "bitter" to "belief"? Do you need a question answered? Do you just need to talk to somebody?**]

NOTE: Be careful. Students who are a grieving a devastating loss don't want or need to be told how to feel. Pray that grieving students would feel God's compassion for and acceptance of them in this session.

PUT ON THE PROMISES OF GOD

Students redecorate their Garbage Garbs with symbols of their relationship with God.
Break into small groups. Discuss the following questions:

- On your own journey of trying to make sense of your life, what character do you identify with most: Naomi, Ruth, or Orpah? Who would you most like to identify with?
- What has been the toughest loss or tragedy you've ever had to deal with in your life?
- God knows everything we're going through. We were never meant to walk through this tough life without the comfort of a relationship with Him. If you really believed that God had an outstretched, helping hand towards you, what would want to ask of Him? What is it that you need most? *journal*

> **Biblical FAST FORWARD** *Nothing could stop Ruth from pursuing her new faith to the fullest. Her rejection of the murderous gods of her clan, her clean break from the past, and her complete loyalty to her new nation and new God led later rabbis to call her the "perfect proselyte."*

Depending on the maturity of your group, you may want to suggest that they pray for each other now.

[VARIATION: These last two questions are difficult. If your students haven't yet developed a vulnerability with each other, you may want to offer them instead an opportunity to write anonymous answers on index cards. Depending on what's best for your group, they can keep the cards to themselves, turn them into you as prayer requests, or be placed into a box and be pulled out by blind draw by secret prayer partners.]

Tell students that throughout the series they'll get a chance to evaluate the consequences of each woman's decision. In particular, students will see first-hand as the series unfolds that God honored Ruth for her No Return decision to enter Israel. (See Biblical Fast-Forward above.) Say: **At the heart of our deepest crisis, God can be trusted. More than that, God can be leaned on in tangible, concrete ways. Those that learn to trust God when life gets tough will find out that He wants to fill us up with more incredible stuff than we've ever experienced before. He wants to use the tragedies of our life to bring us closer to Him.** (See Optional Extra.)

Have students put their now blank Garbage Garbs back on again. Pass out scissors and copies of Resource 2, "The Good Stuff." Have students snip a few of the phrases that mean the most to them about their relationship with God, and then tape them to their bags. If you want, reintroduce the pile of magazines you've brought in and let them look for pictures that symbolize their relationship with God as well. Leave students with this challenge: **Everything you own and everything that's important to you can someday be stripped away from you. But nothing can ever separate you from the love of God. The question is: Have you ever experienced God in such a way that you have to say, "That's enough for me! You can take all my stuff away, but my friendship with God makes me feel full!"**

If anyone in your group has a particularly weighty struggle on their heart, pray for him or her. Close the meeting by thanking God for His presence and friendship in both the good and bad times of our lives.

>
> **OPTIONAL TAKE ONE EXTRA** *Screen the song "Ironic" (from Alanis Morisette's CD, Jagged, Little Pill) for appropriateness for your group. Morisette is the quintessential jaded 90's rocker. You couldn't find a better song than "Ironic" to sum up this generation's bitter, cynical outlook on life if you wrote one yourself. The song includes sound bytes like "[Life] is like a free ride when you've already paid" and "a traffic jam when you're already late." Play the song and discuss:* **Do you ever feel like this singer does about life—a little cynical about the fact that "life has a funny way of helping you out"? If so, why? If not, why not? How does this song compare to the take on life most of the people at your school have? Do you see any similarities between this singer and Naomi? What are they? What do you think God would say to Alanis Morisette if He had her undivided attention?** *Tell students to stay tuned for the rest of this series to see how God deals with bitter circumstances.*

Assignment—
Read through Chap. 2 at least twice this wk + write down any ?s, thoughts etc.

Ruth

Crisis Point: When you call the hot-line, say:
I'm basically a helpless, hopeless widow grieving over the death of my husband. I have a choice: I can either follow my penniless, depressed mother-in-law into a strange country where I'll be hated and have little or no chance of ever being married again. Or I can turn around and go back where I came from. What should I do?

Quick Facts:
- The best thing about Israel is their God doesn't require child sacrifice. You want to learn more about this God.
- In Israel, you'll be quite poor and have "bag lady" status.
- You really have no place to go, though, in Moab, either.

Orpah

Crisis Point: When you call the hot-line say:
I'm just a helpless, hopeless widow and I can't take it anymore! I lost my husband and I don't have a penny to my name. My bitter mother-in-law is driving me crazy and I've got to get out of here. I want to go back home to Moab. Do you think that's a good decision?

Quick Facts:
- Since you've been hanging out with your mother-in-law, you've been learning a lot about her God. What you're learning makes a lot of sense, but it's getting too tough to deal with this loss without your family.
- Back home in Moab, you have a strong support system of family and friends. They don't know anything about this God of Israel, but even the "same-old, same-old" is better than this!

Naomi

Crisis Point: When you call the hot-line say:
I'm just a helpless, hopeless widow. I've also lost my two sons recently. I can't help but feel angry and bitter towards God. Look at my awful life! Everything's ruined. I have two great daughters-in-law, but I have nothing to offer them. I wish they would just go away and leave this bitter, old lady alone. Should I ditch my daughters-in-law, or what?

Quick Facts:
- You've decided to move back to Israel because you have relatives and property there and the drought is over.
- Not only can you kiss your chances of being married again good-bye, with no sons, your hopes of passing on your name are all but dead.

My life has meaning and purpose.

I'm storing up treasures in heaven.

Write your own:

I'M LOVED. NO MATTER WHAT.

JESUS MADE A NO RETURN DECISION TO PURSUE A RELATIONSHIP WITH ME.

I've been redeemed!

GOD is my rock.

He is my strength.

Write your own:

Jesus died for me.

There is quality in my friendships.

God carries me when I need Him most.

I KNOW WHERE I'M GOING.
I HAVE DIRECTION.

I don't have to walk through life alone.

I AM **SOMEBODY** BECAUSE OF MY IDENTITY IN CHRIST.

Write your own:

I will always have a friend.

God comes through. EVERY TIME.

God responds to my small steps of faithfulness with huge steps back to me.

God forgives me.

POWER.

Forever Friends

PROFILE

Ruth and Naomi: What a combination! Forced together into the worst of circumstances by the most discriminating of laws, their journey to Israel could have easily been made into a class-B horror flick: "*Road Trip*: She's the mother in law, she's whining and complaining, and you're stuck with her!" As members of arch enemy Near-Eastern tribes, the potential for culture clashing and values smashing was way high. But a funny thing happened on the way to Israel. They got along. In fact, they went from foreigners to Forever Friends. Though no Super Believer (we saw her carry around a chip on her shoulder in Session 1), Naomi introduced Ruth to the Lord. God's presence in their friendship helped them overcome differences in background and personality. As a result, instead of combat they had commitment. Instead of bickering, they had blessings. And in the midst of overwhelming grief, they carried each other's burdens. Because of her No Return commitment to Naomi, Ruth still stands up today as a powerful role model for godly friendship.

KEY POINT

Be a No Return friend.
Self-centered friendships crumble under stress. But faith in God is a serious bond. Make a bold move. Let your friends know you're a teammate for the long haul.

TOOLS

step 1
• Crepe paper
• Tape
• *Optional Extra:* Cardboard (3 pieces, approx. 1' x 1' ea.)

step 2
• Paper and pens
• Hole punch
• Yarn

step 3
• *Variation:* lab coat, glasses, fake beard, wig, newsprint, markers, pointer

• Copies of Resource 3
• Copies of Resource 4

step 4
• Paper and pens
• Hole punch
• Yarn
• Optional Extra: paper, markers

step 5
• Heavy stock paper
• Pile of crayons and markers

 step 1 **ELECTRIC FENCING**

Students kick off the lesson by participating in an initiative game.
Before students arrive, tape a large piece of crepe paper shoulder high in whatever doorway students have to enter to get to your youth room. As students arrive, tell them you will start the lesson when everyone makes it over the electric gate (represented by the crepe paper). They can not go under, around, nor touch the crepe paper. Once a person is over the gate, they may not return to the original side until all students make it across safely. (See Optional Extra.)

When the entire group has made it across, find some way to encourage each student. Praise the one who had good ideas, the one with the best attitude, the girl who worked through her fears, the guy who wanted to give up but didn't, etc. Use the following questions as a guide to discussing the dynamics of the group interaction.

- **Did anyone try to make it over (or across) alone? What was that like?**
- **How did this task require everyone to work together?**
- **What were some of the drags that kept you from coming to a quicker solution?**
- **What happened when some of you took an independent attitude? Or when others of you thought, "I'm not important"?**

[VARIATION: Larger groups may need to subdivide with two or more teams running the same challenge in two places. Consider having multiple discussion facilitators, as the dynamics of each team will be different.]

 step 2 **HOW TO LOSE FRIENDS**

Students author the book How to Lose Friends *and compare notes with Naomi.*
The exercise we just learned about can teach us a lot about friendships, but let's pretend for a minute that we don't want to build good friendships. Let's say we want to author the book *How to Lose Friends and Influence Nobody.* What good . . . I mean, bad advice would you offer up

---

OPTIONAL TAKE ONE EXTRA

If you can't pull off the electric fence, try this game instead: Give your group three pieces of cardboard, big enough for only one person to step on at a time. Tell them the floor has become a sea of poison that kills on contact, even through shoes and clothes. The only way to get to the other side is to use the cardboard. (Like above, the lesson starts when all students arrive at the other side, but this time students can go back and forth as needed as long as they don't touch the floor without the cardboard.)

for such a book? Pass out paper and pens and have each student write down one or two tidbits of advice on the most effective way to destroy friendships and squander relationships. For example, students might write something like: Announce your friend's most embarrassing moment over the school intercom; when your friend starts eyeing somebody in Geometry class, whisper rumors about them until they're spread all over school; or, when introduced to your friend's parents, belch loudly and say "Yo, dude w'sup?" Read as many submissions as you have time for. If you want, use a hole punch and yarn to string these quips together into a "book."

Then, moving into a review of Session 1, say: **It seems to me that Naomi was out to write the book** *How to Lose Friends and Influence Nobody* **long before we were. Do you remember how she went about it?** As needed, remind students that Naomi was first widowed, and second watched her two sons die as well. Ask: **What do you remember about the way Naomi treated her daughters-in-law?** Then have students scan Ruth 1:1-15, 20, 21. See if they can pick out all the friendship-busting tips from Naomi's example. Add these tips to your book. Supplement your students' answers with the following as needed:

- *Throw a pity party for yourself.* Like Naomi, spend all your time whining and complaining about how bad your life is. This is an efficient way to make those around you sick of you in the shortest amount of time possible.
- *Treat the people who love you like dirt.* Like Naomi, if friends remain loyal to you even as you wallow in self-pity, show absolutely no gratitude. Insist that you're a loser. Demand that they go away. Nobody can stay friends with you long in that kind of environment.
- *Fester in bitterness and make no effort to heal.* Like Naomi, focus all your energy on hating what God has done to you and remember: never, ever, ever ask for God's comfort. The longer you can hang out in the house of bitterness, the more certain you are to be of no value to anyone.
- *Convince yourself that you have nothing to offer.* Like Naomi, work hard at seeing an ultimate loser whenever you look in the mirror. Be careful—if, by chance, you do see some strength in yourself, you might actually learn to use your strength to help others. And that would be dangerously close to *being* a friend.
- *Wait hopelessly for Prince Charming or Cinderella.* Like Naomi, place all your value on romantic love. Regard your same-sex friendships like some kind of booby prize. If you happen to not be dating anyone at the time, bury your head in the sand. If your friends haven't bolted yet, they will when they don't feel valued.

Ask:
- If someone were to write a book based on how you handled your friendships, what would be a good title for it?
- Which tips from the book *How to Lose Friends* do you find yourself following most closely? In other words, what are your favorite ways to push friends away?

Well, Naomi field-tested the friendship-busters in her new book on her daughters-in-law, and it seemed to work pretty well—on Orpah at least. What do you think Orpah felt after Naomi treated her like that? What do you think their good-bye scene looked like? (See Optional Extra.)

Have students work in pairs or small groups to write the dramatic good-bye scene between Naomi and Orpah for the forthcoming Hollywood remake of Ruth. Maybe Naomi says, "Just go back! Leave me alone!" Maybe Orpah responds with something like "Fine! Maybe I will then!" If you have a couple of students who could pull off this sort of thing, you might have them act out the scene.

step 3 DIAGNOSIS: "CINDERELLA COMPLEX"

Students get free friendship checkups at a Dr. Sy Cole Babble "seminar."
Introduce the next step by saying: **Well, Naomi's depression was getting worse and something had to be done about it. It might be too late to take her to the doctor, but we can sure take the doctor to her. It's my very special privilege to introduce to you the esteemed psychologist Dr. Sy Cole Babble, who will give us a full evaluation of Naomi's condition.** If you can, have a volunteer play the part of Dr. Babble, a highly esteemed psychologist. Or, quickly slip behind a door and make it obvious to your students that you've come back "in character."

[*VARIATION*: Slip into a wash room and come out in full costume. Any number of props can help you pull off the identity switch: a white lab coat, glasses, a fake beard, an Einstein-esque wig, etc. If you're willing to fully immerse yourself in character, you might come out sporting a new, sophisticated European accent of some kind. To complete the gag, you might want to hang two newsprint posters, outlines or sketches of two female characters, Naomi and Ruth. Bring a pointer and use the posters as diagrams as you relay your diagnoses.]

As Dr. Babble, say: **Upon careful examination, I, in my expert opinion have come up with the diagnosis for Miss Naomi . . . She has an acute case of the "Cinderella Complex!"** Pass out copies of Resource 3, "Cinderella Complex," which not only explains the causes and symptoms of this mental disorder but also gives students a chance to evaluate their own at-risk level. The "Cinderella Complex" is based on the idea that like Cinderella, we're ugly and unvalued until our Prince Charming comes along. This is an attitude that, especially at the high school level, can be quite common. Students often judge their self-worth based on the popularity and attractiveness of their boyfriend/girlfriend. Not having a boyfriend or girlfriend is often considered a state of absolute disgrace. Naomi expressed this attitude as well by calling her life worthless and forgetting what she had in her friendship with Ruth.

Using the resource as a guide, you can continue to expound from your vast knowledge on this disorder, or let students read about it themselves. When the group has had ample time to fill out the sheet, move next into a diagnosis of Ruth. Remaining in character, say: **Now, this Ruth character is a bit more, how shall we say, tricky to diagnose. In all my years of study, I've never seen someone so willing to give, and yet not receive . . . to be strong and yet not tire of her friend's weaknesses. Any psychologist worth his spit knows: human relationships are based on the gold-plated rule—you scratch my back and I'll scratch yours. But the way Ruth treats Naomi confounds every modern psychological principle! I have named this condition NoReturnisItis. In her friendship with Naomi, Ruth has passed the point of No Return! . . . NoReturnisItis has a strong chance of becoming, what is the word, contagious, if we're not careful. That's why I'm passing out to you this "Friendship Checkup" so that you can evaluate the No Return level of your own life.** Pass out copies of Resource 4, "Friendship Checkup" and give students a few minutes to evaluate the No Return quality of their own friendships.

Disuno Friendship Checkup

Disuno Friendship Checkup ↙

18

step 4 WORKS EVERY TIME

Students author the book, How to Keep Friends.

Referring to the book students wrote in Step 2, say: **Now that we're such experts on friendship after listening to Dr. Babble's seminar, we're ready to author a different book. This time we'll write:** *How to Keep Friends and Make a Difference in Their Lives.* Rescan Ruth 1:9-18 and tell students to pay special attention to Ruth's seven vows in verses 16 and 17. Sticking as closely as possible to what they've read in this session on Ruth and Naomi, have students work in pairs or small groups to contribute tidbits of practical friendship advice to this new book. Pass out pens and paper and tell students the advice they submit can be either serious ("No matter how tough things get, stay committed,") or humorous ("If any of your friends ever want to end your friendship, just wrap them up in a huge bear hug and don't let go"). Supplement student answers with the following:

- ***Where God leads, go.*** Ruth's No Return commitment to follow God put her in a place where there was no backing out of her friendship with Naomi. No matter what. Unlike self-centered friendships that crumble under stress, Ruth and Naomi were actually able to weather their time of turmoil and reap the benefits. Surviving the stress together made them forever friends.
- ***Refuse to lose.*** Ruth was able to put up with Naomi's junk because she kept focus on where she had been and where she was going. She remembered what Naomi's friendship had meant to her in the good times, and that allowed her to give to Naomi unselfishly in the tough times. Ruth knew that Naomi would help her find a strong relationship with the living God of Israel, and that gave Ruth something to anchor her commitment in.
- ***Put your friendship where your mouth is.*** Anybody can talk a good game about friendship. When your friends are down, discouraged, and dumping on you, that's your best chance to show what kind of friend you really are. Ruth put her friendship on the line with seven No Return commitments.

Ask:

- **What one or two tips are you taking home from this book to apply to your own friendships?**
- **In general, how good are you at being a No Return friend even when your friends become bitter, depressed and start dumping on you for a season?** (See Optional Extra.)

Ruth expressed her friendship to Naomi with seven No Return commitments. Encourage students to express their commitments to each other. Pair off into "prayer partners." For the sake of numbering evenly, allow as many as three in one group. Have students commit to getting to know and praying for one another.

journal

OPTIONAL TAKE ONE EXTRA

Give each teen one sheet of paper and toss a bunch of colored markers in the center of the group. Have the teens write the word "ME" on one side of the paper in any way they think describes them and then decorate around the "ME" with things that remind them of themselves. When all are done share the creations. On the reverse side of the paper: 1) In the upper left corner have teens list three "-ing" words that describe their best friend. 2) In the upper right corner have teens list three "-ing" words that describe what they think the perfect friend would be. 3) In the lower left corner have teens list three "-ing" words that describe Jesus as a friend. 4) In the lower right corner have teens list all "ing" words that appear more than once. Compare the words for Jesus and the perfect friend, Jesus and their best friend, and Jesus and words they would use to describe themselves. Discuss the similarities and differences. Then have a dedication ceremony committing to growth in godly friendships with Jesus as one's model and friend.

step 5 TAKE AN OFFERING

Students count what they have to offer and encourage other group members.
In review of the differences between Naomi and Ruth, say: **When Naomi took inventory of her life, she counted what she didn't have, what she wasn't able to give, and all the ways that she was a burden to her friends. Not a good friendship strategy. On the other hand, Ruth took inventory of her life and made a No Return decision to give up everything she had. She became somebody her friends could count on.**

Have students affirm in each other what they have to offer. Say: **Naomi had a lot to offer. She may not have had much in the way of material wealth. But she still had the wisdom gained from her experience. She could teach Ruth what it meant to love God. She could help Ruth find her way in a new country with new customs. Naomi had a lot to give, but she couldn't see it. I don't want to let you guys miss what you have to offer.** (See Biblical Fast-Forward.)

 Although Naomi's bitterness often affects the way she is able to convey her friendship and thanks to Ruth, in Ruth 4:15 the townspeople recognize Ruth's love and character. With Naomi's praise, they say Ruth is better than seven sons.

Provide each student with a card (any piece of folded stock paper will do) and a pile of crayons or markers. Give them a few minutes to decorate the front of the card with their name, decorations, and a list of some of the best things they have to offer their friends. Students can list words like loyalty, commitment, etc., or statements like "I am the kind of person my friends can listen to." Then break down into small groups and have students pass their cards around the group. You may want to travel around to each small group and sign as many cards as you can. Your opinion will no doubt be highly valued. For each card, have small group members write an answer to the following question: **Based on what you know of this person, what do you see as some of the best strengths they have to offer their friendships?**

Say: **The biggest thing that Naomi missed was that she had a wealth of things to offer in a friendship because God was in her life.**

Discuss:
- **What kind of things do you have to offer to your friends as a Christian that non-believers might not have to offer?**
- **What does a Christ-centered friendship really look like? Are your friendships more Christ-centered or self-centered? How would you like them to be?**

 The best way for students to learn about what a Christ-centered friendship looks and acts like is to see one in action. If there is a friend in your life you can bring to the meeting, now would be a great place to have the two of you talk about the difference that the presence of Christ makes in your friendship.

In closing, celebrate the fact that when Christian friendships hit tough times there's a Higher Source to tap into for strength. (See Optional Extra.) Have students pray in small groups for their friendships.

*Assignment
Read Chap. 1 at least twice this wk.
getting down ?s, thoughts etc.
Keep track of what you're offering your friends.*

"Cinderella Complex"

The "Cinderella Complex" is a psychosomatic dating disorder severely affecting one's self-esteem. Most patients who have this disorder convince themselves their life is meaningless without a boyfriend or girlfriend.

SYMPTOM 1. Check off any of the following warning signs that you may be ignoring all of your other friends to spend time with your "romantic interest":

❏ Your idea of quality time with your friends is talking about how great your last date was.

❏ It's not like you monopolize conversations with your friends. Sometimes you let *them* talk about how great your boyfriend or girlfriend is.

❏ Other friends? You can't even remember the names of any of your friends.

❏ With numerous friends of the same sex, you still feel lost or depressed without your "significant other."

❏ You haven't spent any time with any of your other friends in over a week.

SYMPTOM 2. How to tell that you may be a little too desperate for a date:

❏ When Sally tells you she can't go out with you because she has to "wash her hair," you call back an hour later to see if she's done yet.

❏ The last time you were stuck at home alone on Friday night, you tried your best to make the most of it. You stuck in a tape of *The Little Mermaid* and cried all the way through it. (Hey, that final scene is a real tear-jerker!)

❏ When out with your friends, you just can't enjoy it no matter how hard you try because it's not a "date".

❏ You agree to do anything to get a date, even bungee jump from the Eiffel Tower.

❏ Your world would be completely destroyed if you did not have a date to the prom.

SYMPTOM 3. You may be taking your break-up too hard if any of these events occur:

❏ You lock yourself in the closet for two weeks.

❏ You date somebody "on the rebound" just to make your "ex" jealous.

❏ You are found walking around the school hallways in a daze mumbling "My life is over."

❏ You vow never to get out of bed again and stay there until firefighters come and pull you out.

IF YOU HAVE ANY OF THESE SYMPTOMS, TAKE THIS CONDITION SERIOUSLY. APPLY THE FOLLOWING REMEDY ONLY AS DIRECTED:

1. DATE OR NO DATE, COUNT WHAT YOU DO HAVE.
2. VALUE YOUR FRIENDS.

On a scale of 1-10, I struggle with my self-esteem if/when I'm not dating anyone:

1 2 3 4 5 6 7 8 9 10

On a scale of 1-10 I feel completely content with relationship with God and my friends.

1 2 3 4 5 6 7 8 9 10

Friendship Checkup

Take your vital signs.

When my friendships face stress:

❏ They crumble like a house of cards.

❏ It's difficult for me to know how to handle it.

❏ I close my eyes, hold my breath, and try to wait out the storm.

❏ I step up and do what it takes to be a No Return friend.

When my friends are "needy":

❏ I run from them as fast as I can.

❏ I don't hang with them as much until they "get it together."

❏ I try to help, but I'm often drained and depressed by them.

❏ They know that they can count on me.

The song that best describes my friendships is:

❏ I'll Be There For You.

❏ Lean On Me, But Not Too Hard.

❏ Friends are Friends Forever, So Let's Talk About It Later.

❏ When The Going Gets Tough, I'm Outta Here.

The last time I took a huge risk and made a bold move for one of my friends was:

_____

_____

_____

In my closest friendships, Christ is:

❏ The Center

❏ The Silent Partner

❏ The Mystery Guest

❏ The Nowhere Man

Make the diagnosis.

On a scale of 1-10, I would rate the No Return quality of my closest friendships:

1   2   3   4   5   6   7   8   9   10

Make a prescription.

If I really had a No Return attitude towards my friendships, two things I would do differently are:

1. _____

2. _____

One thing I can do this week to be a better No Return friend Is: _____

PROFILE

Ruth's No Return decision to up and leave her old lifestyle wasn't about to get easier now that she reached Israel. After all, to her new neighbors Ruth was one of those evil, God-forsaking, Jew-robbing, baby-killing, ever-attacking Moabites. Let's face it: she couldn't even babysit for a buck.

Like a bag lady rumbling through an alley trash bin, Ruth had to "glean" to eat. She had to scrape up the "trash" crop accidentally dropped by the grain harvesters. (Guess what's for dinner? Bread . . . again!) Life had taken her to the gleaners, but not for long. A hopeless, helpless widow slumming in the grain fields? This is a job for . . . God's church. A wealthy landowner named Boaz took Ruth under his wing, showering her with kindness and provision. "Church" may be a New Testament term, but it's always been God's plan to use His faithful followers as instruments of His kindness and provision. The story of Ruth and Boaz can teach us a lot about what God designed the church to look like "in the flesh."

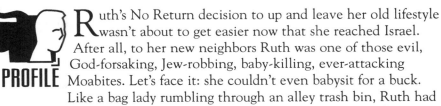

KEY POINT

Flesh out the church.
God is calling His faithful followers to be His hands and feet. To see hurting, left-out people through His eyes. To put flesh and bones on His vision of the church.

TOOLS

step 1
• *Optional Extra:* canned goods, collected blankets; or, TV, VCR, clips from a movie or documentary on videocassette tape showing real-life scenes of homeless, poor, or rejected people

step 2
• Copies of Resource 5 and pens

step 3
• *Optional Extra:* TV, VCR, pre-recorded skit on videocassette tape
• Confetti or a pile of small paper scraps

step 4
• Paper and pens

step 5
• Large piece of posterboard, paste, tape, pens, scissors, magazines, newspapers
• *Optional Extra:* Copies of Resource 6

If it all possible, you may want to begin your meeting with a field trip: bring canned goods to a homeless shelter, pass out blankets to homeless people, or participate in some other service project that might expose teens to some of the poor and "left-out" people in your city. If you'd rather arrange a service project for an entirely different day, consider showing clips from a movie or documentary that shows real-life scenes of homeless, poor, or rejected people. This kind of activity will get students thinking not only of their own experiences of being left out, but of those who have bottomed out and seem to be left out of society as a whole.

step 1 BLOCK OUT

Students play a variation of "Red Rover" called "Block Out."

Make two teams and play "Block Out." a variation of the childhood game "Red Rover." (Or see Optional Extra.) Have each team huddle together and lock elbows, facing inward. When an opposite team member's name is called, that person has ten seconds to try to break into the opponents' circle before having to return to his/her own team. The circled team members try to block such an intrusion. If the player breaks in, he/she can take one player back to his/her team. If the player fails to break in under thirty seconds, he/she must become a part of the new team. As a group, discuss what it feels like to be blocked out, left out, or just plain out of touch. To get the discussion rolling you might ask questions like:

• **What does it feel like to be left out or unable to fit in?**
• **When you're "blocked out" in real life, how do you try to get in?**

step 2 DOWN AND OUT

Students create plans for welfare reform and vote on the best one.

What you're looking for is a creative way to introduce the topic: How does God deal with society's "forgotten" people. One option for achieving this end would be to bring in a volunteer that is disguised as a homeless street person. Of course, this should be a friend of yours from outside your church or someone else your students wouldn't recognize. Explain that you've brought this person to the group so that he can get cleaned up and get something to eat. Feed him whatever snack food you might have lying around the room, watch how students react, and then after a few minutes have him insist that he must be going. If you're able to pull off this simulation effectively, your teens will probably experience a variety of emotions. Pick their brains for reactions. Give them an open floor to talk about what they're thinking and feeling, from: "Why didn't you take him home with you?" to "Why does God allow people's lives to bottom out like that?" Then, affirm students that their emotions are legitimate but tell them the truth about this situation. Say: **I wanted you guys to get a real, legitimate feel for what it's like to face someone who doesn't have a lot. I wanted you to wrestle with what that feels like, and you all were very sincere. Even though this situation wasn't real today, we know that real people in real situations live like the person we met today.**

[VARIATION: You might choose instead to have a couple of your most impressive thespians act out a dialogue of a bag lady and a homeless man talking about their life, or a monologue of the same theme. Instead of giving them a script to follow, have them ad lib what they think a person might say, think, and feel in that situation, including the feeling of being left out and abandoned by God.]

As you switch gears, ask: **True or false: Some people are left out in life. God forgets some people. Sometimes, even in God's kingdom, people fall through the cracks. They end up on the streets or somewhere else, alone.**

Follow up by asking students who think the above statement is false: **Then what do you say to somebody who's got nothing? What do you say to somebody who's life has unraveled and who looks in real life like the person we met today?**

Any way around it, this is a difficult subject to tackle. Chances are, teens will have as few answers here as you do. The goal is that by the end of the session, you will help give teens hope that there is a place for everyone in God's kingdom.

Divide into small groups of three to five, and hand out copies of Resource 5, "Welfare Reform." Give students adequate time to come up with their earth-shattering, world-changing plans in response to the assignment. Have a reporter from each small group outline its plan in front of the rest of the group. If you want, hold a mini-debate over which plan is the best and vote on a winner.

step 3 U.F.O.

Students study God's plan to take care of the needy.
Review the first two sessions. If you can pull off the visual gag in the Optional Extra sidebar, it will make a great way to catch your students up to speed. But for an easier version, try the following: Consider having one of your students role-play a famous TV talk show host. She should introduce her guest, the famous biblical character Orpah, some years after her decision to return to Moab. Prepare your actors in advance. Instruct your host to ask questions about child sacrifice, discrimination against widows and other factors that make life tough in Moab.

Say: **In stark contrast to Orpah, Ruth made a decision to go past the point of No Return. She followed the true God to Israel. Surely, with God on her side, she must be doing better than Orpah. Surely, everything in her life must be good and perfect by now, since she's made the right choice to follow God.**

Then read Ruth 2:1-3. Explain what's going on here: **Hebrew "welfare" was quite different from our modern American system. There were no government handouts, food stamps or Medicare, just the lowest of the low in back-breaking labor. The only way for her to get food was to "glean," to follow behind the grain harvesters in the field picking up the leftover grain behind them. From dawn to dusk she'd labor in the hot,**

Read 2:1-16 through

 An excellent way to accomplish a review of Ruth's story so far might be to videotape one of your teens before the lesson acting as a roving reporter on location in Moab. This reporter should interview Moabite mothers (or students role-playing such) who have had to sacrifice their babies to the god Chemosh (see Biblical Rewind in Session 1). The reporter should talk about other hardships of life in Moab and close with an up-close interview of Orpah, reviewing her decision to return to Moab. Portray Orpah as still having a discouraged, "beaten down" attitude. She should say things like, "Some people, like me, just can't ever catch a break. Life just passes us by. No, Moab's not the best place to be, but you know what—there is no best place to be anymore. Life stinks. That's all there is to it."

Mid-Eastern sun with no rights to water, shade or a sexual harassment suit—she was at the mercy of those hormone-harried male workers looking for some easy prey. In fact, being lower than the servants, she had to beg permission from the top field hand even to scrape the leftovers off the ground. Talk about low and humiliating! And you think flipping burgers for a living is bad. Try this! (If you've mentioned the title of this step to your students, you might want to explain it here—Ruth was an "Unidentified Foreign Oat-picker." OK, so she was probably picking wheat. But what in the world kind of title is "UFW"?)

If you think your students might need a concrete way to relate to Ruth—or if you just need an active break—bring in a bucket of confetti (any stash of tiny, cut up paper pieces will do), spread it over the floor and demand that your students pick it up. Don't offer any rewards. Don't make it a contest. See who complains, who refuses, and who actually complies. Say: **Now imagine that you're Ruth and this is how you get your dinner every night! The confetti would be grain and when you got home, guess what would be for dinner: bread! (Again.)**

This instruction to Jewish landowners not to glean their harvest fields or return for forgotten sheaves is found in Leviticus 19:9 and Deuteronomy 24:19.

Say: **Gleaning was the first part of God's welfare program. Landowners were required by law to leave the leftover grain on the fields for the express purpose of making it available to the widows and the orphans. (See Info Byte.) It required some hard work by the laborers, but it was better than leaving them with nothing.**

Ask:

• **What do you think of this plan? How does it stack up against some of your plans?**

 • **What do you think of Ruth's No Return decision to participate in this plan? What did she risk? What other options did she have?** (See Biblical Rewind.)

You may also want to point out that Ruth's decision to glean—to stay within God's plan—is quite different from Elimelech and Naomi's original decision to move the family to Moab. Read Ruth 2:4-16. (See Info Byte.)

A sojourner was not simply a foreigner or stranger. He was a long-term resident, having moved from his home country. Although all sought acceptance and refuge, some rules did apply. No sojourner could possess land. They shared in the third tithe along with Levites and widows at the city gate. They were not slaves but usually they were in the service of some Israelite in exchange for protection. They were to be treated like an Israelite in being responsible to and protected by the Law (Lev. 19:34).

 • **How would you summarize Boaz's character? How would you summarize the way Boaz treated Ruth?**

• **What impact, if any, do you think Boaz's faith had on the way he treated Ruth?**

Say: **Boaz went way beyond what the law required. He set her up to succeed. He was kind to her and provided for her in ways she could have never earned. Boaz fleshed out the second part of God's plan for the left out. He became the church to her.**

An epaph was about three fifths of a bushel and was some serious take-home pay for just one day in the fields.

• **What do you usually think of when you think of the church?**
• **What do you think about this statement: God has always desired to use his faithful followers as tools for kindness and provision to those in need? Do you agree or disagree?**
• **Do you think it's a good plan? How does it compare to yours?**

BE THE CHURCH

Students brainstorm ways they can flesh out the church in their group.
Review some of the questions that kicked off your study in Step 1: "Are some people in life left out?" etc. See if students have any new and improved answers to add now that they've all become experts on God's plan for "the church" as seen through Boaz and Ruth. (See Optional Extra.) After taking student responses say: **No one need be left out of the kingdom of God. Everyone can be included as a first-class citizen, or more accurately, as a family member. It's the job of God's family to rise up and make themselves available to be instruments of God's provision and kindness to those in need.** (See Optional Extra.)

For this next step, have your students focus on "the church" as it relates first to your own youth group. See if you can challenge your students to take the next step in building community with each other. Pass out paper and pencils and have students write answers to the following questions: **How can this group do a better job being the church to me? What do I need that my friends in this group might be able to support me in? What can this group pray for me about? What can this group do for me if I asked?** Tell students they can remain as anonymous with their requests as they wish. If some students feel comfortable sharing their requests out loud, allow time for that to happen. Respond immediately either by praying for that student, making a plan to help him or her, or both.

On a second piece of paper, have students write two more things: First, have them write down a long-term goal of how they can flesh out the church in this group. Goals might be anything from "show more kindness to other group members" or "include Jill in my clique" to "help Rodney with his homework." Secondly, have them write below that a very specific, tangible way to make their suggestions happen. For example, if the student wrote down a goal to be kinder, a specific follow-up might read something like, "I will make my best effort to sit next to Joe in math class and talk to him as a friend."

JIGSAW CHURCH

Students make service project plans and symbolize the church by making a puzzle.
Now, switch your focus from the church in your group, to the church at large. As a group, brainstorm ways that you can either personally or corporately "flesh out the church" in your community. Answers here will be limited only by your students' creativity and your own willingness to implement. You might plan a service project, e.g., serve at a soup kitchen, paint or do other maintenance work for a local charity.

Make a jigsaw puzzle symbolizing God's plan for the church. If you have time before the lesson, make a collage by pasting pictures of people on a large sheet of posterboard. Access magazines like *National Geographic* and be sure your pictures represent a cross section of various nations, races, colors, ages, economic levels, and capabilities. Then, create your "jigsaw puzzle" by cutting the board into a number of odd-shaped pieces. If possible, cut one piece for each student and pass out the pieces. You may want to put

From the "If you have time" files: You may want to foreshadow the rest of God's plan of outreach to the lost: The Kinsman-Redeemer law. Review the law in Numbers 27:11 and then have students discuss one more time how God's plan compares to their plans. You may want to point out that for a Moabitess, being married by a Kinsman-Redeemer was akin to being included in the Kingdom of God.

If your students are rather musical and if you need an infusion of light-hearted fun, try to come up with some theme songs for this chapter of Ruth. A group of guys might sing "Glean on Me" to the tune of "Lean on Me." The girls might come up with a song from Ruth such as "Gleaning on the Everlasting Arms" or a Beach Boys approach with "I'm going to glean, glean, glean, 'til Boaz comes and takes me away."

a piece of double-sided masking tape on the back of each puzzle piece and reassemble the puzzle on a flat wall so that all students can see it. Call up students one by one (first call those with corner pieces, then call other flat edge pieces) and have them put their piece on the wall where they think it best belongs. When they do, have them state one way that they can "flesh out the church" in the coming week. If your puzzle is still unfinished after the first round (in other words, if some students placed their pieces in the wrong spot), choose volunteers and give them thirty seconds a crack to see who can effectively make the pieces of the puzzle fit together first.

[VARIATION: For a quicker, more convenient method, bring in a blank posterboard, a handful of magazines, and tape or glue. Break into small groups and cut the posterboard into jigsaw puzzle pieces so that every group can have one piece. Instruct each group to decorate its piece with pictures and words that represent what they see as God's plan for the church. If you don't have enough magazines, have students simply sign their pieces by writing one specific way they will flesh out the church in the coming week. Using tape and a flat surface as above, have a spokesperson explain why his or her group chose to decorate its puzzle piece the way it did. And then take a shot at reassembling it, following the above method.]

Say: **Like the pieces of this jigsaw puzzle, we all fit together in God's kingdom. We all are accepted as family members in God's church.** (See Optional Extra.) (See Biblical Fast-Forward.)

As students bow their heads for prayer leave silent time for them to ponder the following questions:

- **Where are you gleaning in your life? Where are you out in the fields, working your tail off, waiting for God to come through? Identify that area. Know that you are on the right track. You will be tempted to take an easier route and take care of things on your own. But hang in there. You know that God will come through. Pray right now for the persistence to continue to work hard faithfully.**
- **Who is a Ruth in your life right now? Who is someone you know that has some kind of need? Whose life could you really make a difference in by lending a helping hand? Pray for that person right now and make a silent pact with God just to tell Him what you'll do and when you'll do it.**
- **Who is a Boaz in your life right now? Who is someone who has taken you under his/her wing? Who has been God's hands and feet of provision and kindness to you? Take a second to thank God for that person right now. And make another silent pact that you'll find some way to thank that person this week.**

In closing, pray for the difference God can make through your group.

For an optional ending or a supplement to the jigsaw puzzle idea, pass out copies of Resource 6, "The Herald." In small groups, have students fill in a fictional newspaper story of the difference your students are going to make as they apply the lessons they've learned to flesh out the church. They can draw a picture to go along with their story in the box included on the page. You might want to assign different groups different assignments: one group might write a story about the difference your group will make at school; another group might write about the difference your group will make on your upcoming service project; and one group might write about the difference students will make by serving each other in the youth group.

Ruth is a superb example of God's love and impartiality. Although she belonged to a race often despised by Israel, she was blessed because of her faithfulness to God in her own life and as a vital part in God's plan for the redemption of the world.

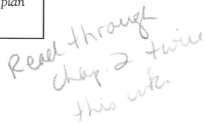
Read through chap. 2 twice this wk.

STAT BOX

America

- 14 million Americans are on the welfare rolls, costing taxpayers $170 billion a year.

- 12% of all Americans and 14.5% of children live below poverty level.

- The total bill for all entitlement programs was over $900 billion in 1995; that figure was projected to jump to 80% of the entire national budget by 2005.

Canada

- From 1988 to 1995, the number of Canadians on welfare jumped from 1.4 million to 3.1 million.

- The welfare program cost taxpayers $14 billion in 1995.

- An average family with a single, unskilled wage earner could make slightly more per year on on welfare than by working at minimum wage. (This is also true in America.)

Overall, I would rate the job my country does with taking care of the poor and needy:

the best in the world   OK

THE BEST WE CAN DO SO FAR

too much dependence on the big government   **I don't have a clue**

The three biggest weaknesses I see in my country's welfare system are:

1.

2.

3.

If I had the chance to design a better system to help take care of the poor and needy in my country some of the significant changes I'd make to the plan are:

THE HERALD

Your Complete News Source

25¢—May vary
outside of metro area

Youth Make Big Impact

PROFILE

Playing the field can be risky business. It was for Ruth. Her mother-in-law Naomi had come up with one of the most wacky matchmaking schemes ever recorded in history. In another bold move, Ruth decided to go along with it. So she powdered her nose, poured on the perfume, and walked through the grain fields. Risking her life, bodily harm, rape, and possible rejection, Ruth passed the sleeping, sweaty bodies of the field workers and sneaked into Boaz's "bedroom," the threshing floor. Dressed in her finest clothes, Ruth lay down next to the man's stinky feet. Ruth waited. And waited. And waited. Startled half to death, Boaz finally realized she was there and awoke . . . with cold feet. Because Ruth held out for the right guy, did things the right way, and waited for the right time, this love connection actually worked. Who says the Bible doesn't talk about dating?

KEY POINT

Stop looking for a great date. Be a great date.
You can't become an overnight charmer if you don't have the right stuff in your heart. God's plan for dating is not always easy. It requires tough choices and bold moves. But He has a plan to give you a great dating relationship.

step 1	**step 3**
• *Variation*: furniture, newsprint, markers	• Pens and paper
• *Optional Extra*: bowls, cereal, orange juice, bread, peanut butter, barbecue sauce, cabbage, salad dressing, forks, spoons, blindfolds	**step 4**
	• Copies of Resource 8, scissors
• *Variation*: TV, VCR, pre-recorded interviews on videocassette tape	**step 5**
	• Newsprint or eraserboard, marker
	• Pens and paper

 step 1 # THE LOVE CONNECTION

Students role-play a version of the TV show, The Love Connection.
Stage your own "Love Connection" game. Introduce your host, Chuck (who can be a student, or you can play the part yourself) and then choose a "contestant"—an unsuspecting female volunteer from your audience who will henceforth be known as "Ruth." (Or see Optional Extra.)

[VARIATION: When students enter, have the room arranged to look like *The Love Connection* set. Set up two love seats or plain chairs facing each other in a "stage" area at the front of your room, and arrange the other chairs around this set where your "audience" will sit. You can further spice up the set with a Love Connection banner that you draw on newsprint.]

You'll need to prepare three males ahead of time, whom your host will interview as potential dates for Ruth. Introduce Ruth's would-be Love Connectors as:

- **SAMSON.** During his interview he could say something like: "I've got a pretty buff bod, man. Don't you think? But I have to say something up front: I don't date girls that mess with my hair. That ain't gonna cut it! My dates will get to wear exotic new attire. But they have to be able to cook health food."
- **GIDEON.** During his interview he might say: "I really want a date with you. I mean, I think so. But I'm not sure I should be on this show. I need a sign from God. OK, God, if I'm supposed to go out with this girl, send a bolt of lightning down from the sky and burn this rug I'm standing on!"
- **BOAZ.** During his interview have him say: "My ideal date is a moonlit walk through the grain fields," and "I'm just looking for a kind, godly woman."

Have the studio audience vote on who they think would make the best date for Ruth. Then see if that matches your Ruth's opinion. Say: **Today we're going to read about how Ruth and Boaz got to cookin' up some romance.** Ask:

- **What do you think of Ruth and Boaz as an "item"?**
- **Based on what you know of them so far, how do you think their romance might turn out?**
- **Does Boaz seem like a pretty cool guy to date? Why or why not? What about Ruth?**

 Introduce the topic of No Substitutions, which is prevalent in this session. Play a game in which you make substitutions in simple recipes and have blindfolded volunteers try to guess what's been substituted. You might try pouring orange juice in a bowl of cereal, put barbecue sauce in place of jelly on a peanut butter sandwich, and/or replace lettuce with cabbage in a salad. How easy is it for your students to tell the difference? Begin to discuss: **What are some "substitutions" in real life that can bring severe consequences?**

[*VARIATION*: The above scenario might not be as funny if your students haven't yet committed the book of Judges to memory. If your students think Samson is some kind of luggage salesman and Gideon is that guy who puts Bibles in hotel rooms, simply take the Love Connection roleplay back to the future. Ahead of time, videotape three females roleplaying familiar youth culture characters (Whitney Houston, Courtney Cox from the TV show *Friends*, and Sandra Bullock are a few examples) answering questions like: What are your interests, hobbies, and special talents? What is your impression of the ideal man? What is an ideal date? Choose a male contestant from the audience, show the video clips and instruct the audience to choose which girl would make the best date for your contestant. Let your contestant choose which of the three characters he would date and tell the audience why. Continue with a second round to tie the activity in to the lesson. Introduce two students you have prepared ahead of time to enter playing Ruth and Boaz, former Love Connectors returning to tell Chuck how their date went down. Have Chuck poke and prod the couple with questions like, "So, did anything romantic happen, or what?" But have the two respond based on what really went down in Ruth 3. (Boaz might say, "Well, I was with her last night, but nothing happened. In fact, I didn't even know she was there most of the night." Ruth might say, "It's hard to be romantic when you've got these big, odorous feet sticking in your face all night.")]

OPTIONAL TAKE ONE EXTRA *Have students shut their Bibles and take a couple of guesses as to what Naomi's game plan might be for the set up. Also, have some students volunteer stories of either how they were set up to date somebody, or set somebody else up on a date. As a final activity here, have students break into small groups and brainstorm the best way to ask a girl/guy that most awkward of all questions: "Would you go on a date with me?" Tell students you're looking for a no-fail, creative way to get the attention of their dream dates. (Humorous answers are encouraged.) Vote on the Most Original and Most Likely to Succeed suggestions.*

step 2 THE GAME PLAN

Students compare their own set-up scams with Naomi's.
Have someone read Ruth 3:1, 2. Point out that Naomi seems to still have a bit of a Cinderella Complex; she's still trying to fix Ruth up.

So, Naomi's going to try to play matchmaker between Ruth and Boaz. How do you think she might do it? (See Optional Extra.)

Read Ruth 3:3-6.
* **What do you think of Naomi's plan?**
* **What a place to lie down, next to a man's stinky feet! What's that all about?** (See Info Byte.)
* **If you were Ruth and unfamiliar with this custom, how do you think you would respond to this idea? Why do you think Ruth decides to go along with this crazy plan?** Point out that Ruth was probably not too familiar with this Hebrew tradition, but she went along with the wacko plan anyway. This is one more bold move by Ruth to follow God's plan, not her own.
* **How do you think the plan turns out? Does it work, or does it crash and burn?**
* **What are some of the things that could go wrong with this plan?** If no one gets it, you may want to remind students that Boaz is guarding his newly-harvested grain. Ask your students what they would you do if they woke up in the middle of the night and found an intruder at their feet. And that's not to mention the long walk Ruth had past the field workers, the Hebrew version walking down an alley on the wrong side of town. In the dark. With her best dress and some sweet perfume on.

Info BYTE *Ruth's not being seductive here. (Think about it. Laying by the sweaty, dirty feet of a tired outdoor worker must have been some turn-off.) Rather, Ruth's act was one of submission. It was common for servants to lie at the feet of their master and even share a part of his covering. In entering the marriage bed, the bride was to enter under the covers from the groom's feet as a sign of submission. Ruth was to apply this to the kinsman-redeemer law, thus informing Boaz of his responsibility to find someone to marry her or marry her himself.*

Students discuss how a No Return attitude could affect their dating lives.
At any given time, probably only a minority of your kids will be in dating relationships. All teens, though, need to hear what Ruth and Boaz have to say about dating, whether they store it away for future use or apply it the following Friday night. But, if you're looking for broader application, check out the Optional Extra sidebars.

Give students a few minutes to design their "ideal date." Hand out pens and paper and have students list physical, spiritual, and character traits they want in their date. As a group, see if you can come up with a consensus as to the one or two most important qualities for a potential date. If students remain divided after a few minutes, you may want to list the most popular choices and take a vote.

Say: **Everybody wants an ideal man or ideal woman. But we all know they don't exist. No one is perfect. So what if you had to substitute some of the things on your list? What if you had to choose between one thing or the other? How would you know what would be most important?** For each of the following questions, have students stand on the left side of the room if they like the first option best or the right side if they prefer the second option.

If you had to choose, would you rather date:

An airhead with a great body	**OR**	*A genius with an average appearance?*
A rich date with a boring personality	**OR**	*A penniless date who's a crack up?*
(Girls Only) Brad Pitt	**OR**	*Pearl Jam singer Eddie Vedder?*
(Guys Only) Pamela Anderson	**OR**	*Sandra Bullock?*
(All) A person who loves God deeply but has no social status	**OR**	*A non-believer who happens to be class president?*

Read Ruth 3:7-11. Ask:

- **How do you think Ruth was feeling waiting that long, and smelling those wonderful feet, for all that time?**
- **What do you think impressed Ruth about Boaz and made her willing to take the risks she took? What impressed Boaz about Ruth?**
- **What can you learn about godly dating from this passage?**

Supplement with the following info as needed: Students may be able to realize here that Ruth and Boaz were both godly people. Boaz comments on Ruth's kindness and her noble character. Judging by the way that he has treated his workers (see Ruth 2:4) and Ruth, we know the same about Boaz. In Ruth 3:10 we find out that Ruth was looking for love in all the right places. Instead of chasing young, rich hunks, she was looking for a man of character who could take care of her. (See Optional Extra.)

OPTIONAL TAKE ONE EXTRA

Instead of asking, "What can you learn about godly dating from this passage?" see what other areas students can apply this No Substitutes principle to. Point out that by waiting on God to provide for her (in this case by waiting for "the right guy") Ruth is again showing a No Return attitude. She accepted No Substitutes. Break into three or more teams. Have teams race to come up with mock "Faith Substitute" campaigns for as many aspects of their daily lives as possible. They should create one-sentence slogans for new "products" that would vie to replace true No Return faith. As a campaign model, consider the way margarine markets itself as a substitute for butter and Equal® as a substitute for sugar. Examples of No Return substitute campaigns might include: "Substitute your daily devotional time by listening to a couple of Christian songs—it's much faster and you can do it on the go." Or: "Substitute real repentance with one blanket 'God forgive me' prayer at the end of each day—it's a real time and energy saver." Discuss some of the real consequences that substitutions have in our walk with God.

When you're picking someone to date, remember this: Good looks don't mean much the first time you get in a fight. A great body won't be so attractive if that person treats you like a jerk. If someone's funny or popular, they might be a blast to have around . . . for a while. But sooner or later you're going to want to connect with someone who will help make you a better person, treat you right, and inspire you to love God more. The first principle of No Return dating is No Substitutes. Ruth held out for the right guy. Ruth could have gone after any number of men richer, younger, more attractive than Boaz. But she decided there was no substitute for a man who would treat her right.

Ask: **Does anybody find anything interesting about the fact that here it is, late at night, Ruth's all dressed up and smelling nice and sitting right there at Boaz's feet, and nothing happens?** Students should be able to recognize that Boaz and Ruth's choice not to have sex right there when the opportunity was available was pretty radical. It would definitely be counter-cultural today.

The second No Return principle is No Short Cuts. Ruth and Boaz waited for the right time. They made a decision to honor God with their actions.

Discuss: **What do you think would have happened if Ruth and Boaz would have decided to go all the way that night?** Let students come up with their own answers here, but try to hit on the fact that it probably would have ruined their relationship before it got started. Despite media perceptions to the contrary, most students understand that physical intimacy that's treated casually is quite simply a recipe for severe heartbreak. (See Biblical Fast-Forward.)

 Ruth and Boaz's sexual purity is quite a contrast to their great grandson's well-documented sex and murder scandal. Faced with a similar "no one will know" situation, David gave in to a one-night fling with Bathsheba. While the consequences of Ruth and Boaz's No Short Cut decision was the healthy marriage that was soon to come, the consequences of David's sin was a serious bust. He lost his baby and watched his family unravel. (II Samuel 11.)

Some of your older students might be in serious, long-term dating relationships. Your younger students might still be looking forward to their first date. All teens can always use more encouragement to stay sexually pure in a world where it probably seems they're the only ones trying to do so. Give students a few minutes to wander the room and state to each other what they think are the best reasons to stay sexually pure. (See Optional Extra.)

[VARIATION: Depending on how much time you have, you may want to point out that one more way Ruth and Boaz showed a No Short Cut attitude was by pursuing the other, closer Kinsman Redeemer. Instead of marrying Ruth right off when no one probably would have known or cared about this other relative, Boaz risked the relationship for the sake of his honesty.

Ask:

- **What parts of your dating life (or if you're not currently dating, what parts of the dating life you think you'll have in the future) will a No Return attitude be necessary? Where will it run into the most resistance?**
- **For those of you who are dating now, do you have a No Return attitude? What kinds of risks are you willing to take to stay on the right track and honor God with your decisions?**

 To make the application of this section more broad, point out that Ruth and Boaz refused to take a path that the media and the rest of society today say is a shortcut to happiness. Try to come up with a list of the Top Ten most tempting "shortcuts" students sometimes consider. Besides premarital sex, the list might include playing the party scene as a short cut to popularity, joining a gang as a shortcut to building deep friendships, etc. Discuss some of the consequences of each of those "shortcuts."

- For those of you who aren't dating, in what areas of your life are you prepared to be a man or woman of No Return?]

AN A-MAZING DATE

Students weave their way through a choose-your-own-ending dating maze.

Say: We've left Ruth and Boaz dangling there like a bad soap opera ending. Will the other Kinsman-Redeemer steal Ruth away? What will happen? I can't give away next week's ending. But I can give you a hint that God had big plans for Boaz and Ruth's new relationship. They honored God by doing things the right way, and God honored them by providing them with a great relationship.

Begin a discussion on what might have happened in Boaz and Ruth's "dating relationship" if they didn't do the right thing at any point during their encounter.

- What might have happened if Ruth pursued some younger, richer dude in the first place?
- What would have happened if Ruth and Boaz slept together on that first night?
- What would have happened if Boaz had not informed Ruth about the other kinsman-redeemer and just gone ahead and married Ruth?

Play the "Dating Maze," an interactive game in which students read about the consequences of their own fictional dating choices. Break students up into groups of two to five. Make enough copies of Resource 8, "Dating Maze" for each team. Before the session, cut out the squares and spread them all over the room in various places: taped to window sills, on the floor, or whatever works. Hand each team a copy of Box 1. Have students answer the questions on the bottom of Box 1 and go from there trying to find other boxes as they are led to other clues around the room. In this exercise, students answer hypothetical dating dilemmas and each choice leads them to a different card. Encourage students to take their time. If you think your students might end up answering all the "right" answers because, after all, they're at church, you may want to encourage them to experiment a little with some "bad choices" just to see how the path unwinds in this safe setting.

Afterwards let students disagree with some of the principles that the cards from the maze might have implied. You may want to pick a few controversial statements from the game and get students' opinions:

- Do you think that God really has plans to make your dating relationships full of joy? Why or why not?
- Do you really believe that if you rush things physically in a relationship that it will cause you to start feeling like things are moving too fast?
- Do you think that if you're not following God in a dating relationship, you'll start to feel like something's missing?

The best way to make the above points more powerful is to give concrete examples. Talk about experiences from your life about how God may have blessed Christ-centered dating relationships with major joy. You may want to prepare a few students to talk as well. Interview students that you prepare ahead of time, not just about the good parts of their Christ-centered relationship, but talk possibly to students who have made bad choices and experienced some tough consequences first hand. (See Optional Extra.)

step 5 DESIGNING THE IDEAL DATE . . . ME!

Students set goals for themselves to help them become better future dates.
Break into two groups—guys and girls. When the small groups huddle up, assign them the task of coming up with consensus answers to the questions: **What are the Top Ten things guys look for in a date?** and **What are the Top Ten things girls look for in a date?** When groups give their reports, list these qualities on newsprint or eraserboard. It will be interesting to see what kind of a priority your group puts on "character" after this session. Ask students to give themselves a Dating Rating based on questions like:

- **How is your ability to make the people you are with feel cared for and accepted? Do you typically put people down or encourage them?**
- **Are you more self-centered or others-centered? When push comes to shove, do you make choices based on "What's in it for me?" or "What I can do to help someone out"?**
- **How committed are you to being pure? Do you have a track record of making big mistakes that have burned relationships in the past? Or are you someone your date can trust?**
- **Do you have the right motives for dating? Are you looking for an important person that you can build up, or are you just looking for somebody to "have a good time" with?**

Throw in other questions that you can think of that will help students evaluate whether or not they have the "right stuff." Hand out paper and pens and have students design *themselves* the same way they designed their ideal dates before. Encourage them to note areas where improvement and change are needed to be an "ideal date."

Say: **No matter what happens or doesn't happen in your dating life, you will be better off when you have the right stuff in your heart. Integrity will help you do the right thing. Purity will help you wait for the right time. Patience will help you wait for the right date. So instead of always dreaming about who we'll date, maybe we should dream about what kind of date *we'd* be.**

When students bow their heads to pray, say: **Is there anywhere you've taken a short cut? Is there anywhere that you've accepted substitutes that you shouldn't have? If God brings an answer to your mind as you're reflecting right now, trust that it's the Holy Spirit nudging you to do some business. I just want to remind you that forgiveness is just one prayer away. Healing is a long process, but one that I want to help you with. Feel free to talk to me after the session.** In closing, pray for God to help each student become a more "ideal date."

 Create your own panel of dating experts. Invite some couples in your church to come in as guest panelists. Choose couples that are married and unmarried; that have scarred and unscarred pasts; that have significant stories to tell. Let students ask questions of your panelists "firing line" style.

Dating Maze

Box 1

Attractive people are constantly begging you for a date. You have your pick of almost the whole school. It's decision time. You know you should probably date someone who loves God and will be a partner with you in following Him. But then again, if you made that kind of decision you'd never know what you were missing: should you really discriminate against great dates just because they don't believe what you do? What about those parties and all that action out there?

IF you choose to pursue dating a non-Christian,

FIND BOX 2

IF you choose to make a NO RETURN decision to value your relationship with God and date someone else who does, too,

FIND BOX 5

Box 2

You land a date with the most attractive, most popular member of the opposite sex in your whole school.

Maybe your date treats you right, but maybe not. Maybe you have a great time, maybe not. But whether you're going to play the field or get serious here, you need to decide—Will God remain a priority in your life or not?

Sooner or later, your values are sure to clash on things like parties, sex, church, praying, and priorities. What are you prepared to do when that happens?

IF you choose to get serious about God,

FIND BOX 4

IF you like the non-Christian dating scene too much to quit,

FIND BOX 3

Box 3

Because of the decisions you've made in your dating life, your relationship with God has crashed and burned. That's your choice, but count the cost. You've dissed the Creator of the universe for a fling that on average might last a couple of weeks. Even if you get lucky and land a long-term deal, you still have to face the fact that you've bumped God into second place. You'll have no idea what kind of quality friendships and joy in dating God wanted to put in your life.

DEAD END

Box 4

You've decided to love God with all your heart and still continue to date your non-Christian partner. Good luck! Just maybe you'll be that once-in-million-years "missionary dater" who actually makes a positive difference in their dating partner's life. Maybe you'll win the lottery, too. For the sake of being realistic, let's say that you keep growing closer to God and your date doesn't. It doesn't take a rocket scientist to figure out: you're growing apart. Something has to be done. Will you compromise with God and make Him less of a priority? Or will you dis your date?

IF you think it would be best if you and your partner were "just friends" so that you can continue to follow God with all your heart,

RETURN TO BOX 1

If you're not willing to make that choice,

FIND BOX 3

You hit it off great with your date. You can't believe how cool it is to like somebody not just for their looks but for their character as well. Since you're both Christians, it feels like this has a lot of potential. Quite soon into your relationship, the two of you find yourselves alone. You know this is moving fast, but you can't help it: the sparks are turning into a full-fledged fire. It's decision time. Part of you says getting physical fast is just "an expression of love." But the other part says . . .

**IF you decide to pursue
physical intimacy with your date,**
FIND BOX 6

**IF you decide it would be best to back
off and wait for the right time,**
FIND BOX 10

Suddenly, you find yourself in a relationship you didn't really want. Everything's happening so fast. The physical part has been nice, but maybe too nice. It's become the focus of your relationship in a lot of ways. And now you're feeling pretty strung out, like you just can't relax and be comfortable in the relationship the way you used to. You see your relationship as centered more and more around the physical. You liked it a lot better when your friendship was centered around helping each other grow closer to God.

**IF you decide to recommit
your relationship to God,**
FIND BOX 9

**IF you're thinking,
"So, what's wrong with being
a little physical?"**
FIND BOX 7

Because of the choices that you've made, you now have a mediocre dating relationship. You don't have the same kind of love for God that you once had in your heart. You don't have the same kind of joy you had about your dating partner when things first started. Things can still get better if you work hard. But things between you and God might also head south if you don't do something about it.

**IF you decide that being
mediocre isn't so bad,**
FIND BOX 3

**IF you decide to recommit
your relationship to the Lord,**
FIND BOX 9

**IF you decide that it's time to
break off the relationship,**
FIND BOX 8

Because of the choices you've made, your relationship has busted. The sad thing about this is that God had some great plans for the two of you. The decisions you made that you thought would work for you have turned out to be wrong and harmful. When you break up, it will be hard to remain friends, but try. You both can learn valuable lessons from your experience. Know that God waits for you to return to Him with all your heart, and He still has great plans for you no matter what you've done. Until you turn your heart back over to Him, though this is a . . .

DEAD END

Box 9

The best place to start getting your relationship back on track is by asking God for forgiveness. God is faithful to forgive and provide you with a clean slate to start over. But the decisions you've made will have consequences. Depending on how far away you've gotten, the healing process might be long and painful. You'll have to start making your wrong choices right, whatever that takes. At the same time, you've just opened a door for God to begin to shower on you the joy, the fun and the love He wants you to have.

GO BACK AND EXPLORE OTHER OPTIONS WITH THE TIME YOU HAVE LEFT.

Box 10

You have made some excellent choices in your dating relationship so far. You have found out that No Return dating is not easy, but now you are very thankful for the special dating relationship you have. God has blessed you! If you continue to love God and to commit your relationship to Him, you will find out what great things He has in store for you.

GOOD JOB!

NOW GO BACK TO BOX ONE AND EXPLORE OTHER OPTIONS WITH THE TIME YOU HAVE LEFT.

session five:

It's All in the G.E.N.E.S.

PROFILE

Ruth counted the cost. She made that No Return decision to enter Israel with her eyes wide open. Bold move after bold move. She was willing to do whatever it took, no matter how rough life got. But she could have never expected this. Not in her wildest dreams. Married. Pregnant. And chosen to one day be the great grandmother of Israel's greatest king. Her inclusion into the "in" crowd of Israel came at a high price to Boaz. But her life was never the same. The way Boaz redeemed Ruth, and the way Ruth responded with a complete overhaul of her entire identity, make a perfect picture of what happens in our own lives when Jesus redeems us.

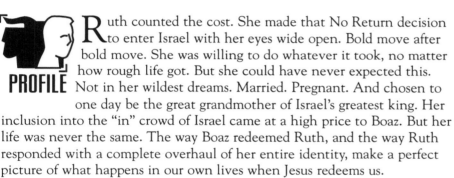

KEY POINT

You've been redeemed. Claim your reward.

Jesus is the ultimate Kinsman-Redeemer and you're the one He bought back. He paid a high price for your freedom. Now you have a completely remodeled identity in Christ. Claim the power. Claim the prize.

step 1
- Table, sheet, thumbtacks or duct tape
- Flashlight
- Scissors
- *Variation:* beakers, books, lab coat, signs
- *Variation:* paper, sheet, laundry makers

step 2
- Can of refried beans
- Canned fruit or pie filling, spoons
- Four to eight more canned food items
- Label from canned dog food

step 3
- Optional Extra: TV, VCR, wedding video
- Pens and paper

step 4
- Drawing paper; pens, markers or paints

step 5
- Copies of Resource 8 and pens
- Scissors
- Party materials: food, music

step 1 — THE FRANKEN-HERO CREATION EVENT

Students help conduct a create-a-hero experiment.

Find a table sturdy enough for a student to lay on, and hang a white sheet in front of it by thumbtacking or duct taping it to the ceiling. Using a lamp, large flashlight, or other portable light source (the brighter the better), shine the light from somewhere behind the curtain to create a shadow effect. Arrange ahead of time for one student to arrive early and have that volunteer laying on the table, identity concealed, when the lesson begins.

[**VARIATION:** When students enter, have the room arranged as much like a science lab as possible. Props like beakers, stacks of books, a white lab coat, signs that read "DANGER: RADIATION," etc. are not essential but will contribute to the atmosphere.]

Kick off the lesson by saying: **Today we will conduct one of the greatest experiments of all-time. We have the technology to build the most godly hero the world has ever seen!**

Ask students how they would design this godly hero, Franken-style. For example, would they choose David's heart? Schwarzenegger's body? Einstein's brain? Or what? Choose a number of characteristics and body parts like this and then announce that the time to operate has come. Go behind the screen and act as if you are operating on your student volunteer. You may want to bring a pair of scissors and make like you are thrusting these into his side, head, or elsewhere. Have the student scream and/or squirm while you do so. Then, with as much fanfare as you can muster, say: **He's ALIVE! The operation was a success! Presenting the most godly hero in all the world!!**

Have the teen then stand up and come out in front of the sheet. Wait for remarks such as: That's no hero! That's so-and-so! etc. Then announce: **Oh, but you are wrong. This may look like just an ordinary, everyday teen, just like you. But this is really the most godly hero the world has ever seen. At least, that's true through God's eyes. God loves to take the ordinary and make it into the extraordinary. Today, we're going to learn that being a "hero" has nothing to do with your "genes." It has to do with the G.E.N.E.S. factor. God Embraces Nobodies and Empowers them to be Somebodies. No matter how messed up your past is. No mat-**

OPTIONAL TAKE ONE EXTRA

For an optional opener, start with the question: **If you were to go into a deep freeze and not wake up for twenty years, what would it shock you the most to find when you finally opened your eyes?** *The idea here is to come up with the most unlikely and "shocking" possible changes, as opposed to predictions. Students can start by making up shocking inventions, developments in technology, or changes in clothes tastes, etc. But the stuff you really want to get at is:* **What would be the wildest change you could imagine taking place in one person?** *Possible answers could include: Howard Stern becomes a Franciscan monk; or, Heather Locklear's career bombs and she becomes a waitress at a local greasy spoon. Ask:* **Does it seem realistic that these changes could take place? What is the most incredible change of identity that you've ever seen?**

ter what your family tree says. God can radically reform our identities. No matter who you are, God has the technology to make a hero out of you.

[**VARIATION**: If you just can't create a curtain, you can accomplish the same skit by having the student lay on the table and covering him with a white sheet. But first, put plain pieces of paper over the volunteer's face, hands, and clothing. Follow the same routine as above, but when students shout out the traits they want in their Franken-hero, use laundry markers to write these traits on the sheet over the appropriate body part. When your hero has been adequately constructed, have the student step out from under the sheet and end this section by reciting the paragraph above.]

step 2 CANNED FOOD DRIVE

Students race to label food cans and then discuss how labels in real life can hurt.
Bring in six to ten canned food items. Before the session begins, open the lids, strip the labels, and place the naked cans at the front of the room in two different sections. Make sure at least one of the cans contains refried beans and another contains something sweet and right-out-of-the-can edible, e.g., fruit cocktail, canned cherry pie filling. Bring an extra label, one from a can of Alpo® or other canned dog food container. Hide the refried beans label in your pocket and sneak the Alpo label in with your pile of other labels.

At this point in the session, divide your group into two teams, hand each team half of the labels and let them race to put the right labels on the right cans. You can do this as a relay: Let each team member run to the front of the room, place or replace one label, and run back to tag their next team-mate until you announce that all the labels are correct. Or, if your group is small enough, turn both teams loose in a mad free-for-all. When the race is over, throw out a couple of spoons and let the winning team have at any of the food they'd like to dig into. While that team goes diving for the pie filling, grab your own spoon and start digging in the refried beans. Since your students will most likely have labeled the beans can with the dog food label, be prepared for some serious gagging and hacking. Before whipping out the true label and spilling the beans on the beans, if you will, offer some to your students and see who turns the palest shade of white. Of course, once your students realize they've been had, you have an excellent segue into a discussion on "labels."

- How is this game like real life? In other words, do we sometimes rush to "label" other people and then find out that we had them all wrong?
- Think about the things you've been labeled in the past. Maybe some of you have heard something like: "You're just a slacker"; "What a loser!"; "You're a quitter" or something similar. How does it feel to be labeled?
- What are some labels that you sometimes hear older people slap on teenagers? Are these labels fair or unfair?
- How do labels affect the way that you act? If someone expects you to act a certain way (like a quitter or a slacker, for example) do you tend to act like they expect? Or do you get mad and "show them"? Or what?

step 3 RUTH, MY HEROINE

Students study how Ruth became a heroine.

Since this session is both a wrap-up and an overview of Ruth's story, rewind to Ruth's original No Return decision and remind students that she knew what it was like to be labeled. By the time Ruth reached Israel, she was a stranger in a strange land. A foreigner. A woman. And a Moabitess to boot. Three strikes against her before she ever came to bat.

 Biblical REWIND *City gates were open places of all sorts of business transactions, buying and selling, and even places where judicial cases were tried and judgments pronounced. This was the place where legal transactions were conducted and witnessed to seal the agreement (Gen. 23:10, 18; Deut. 21:19; 22:15; 25:7-9).*

Ask: **How do you think that affected Ruth? Based on what you remember, how did she deal with it?**

Read Ruth 4:1-12. (See Biblical Rewind.)

- **How do you think Boaz might have felt waiting for the nearest relative to arrive?**
- **What do you think he felt when the kinsman at first said he would redeem the property?**
- **If Ruth had been standing there, what do you think she might have felt?**
- **What do you think the townspeople meant in their blessing?**

Read Ruth 4:13.

- **What do you think Boaz felt at being able to marry such a young and honorable woman?**
- **What do you think Ruth felt about marrying Boaz?**
- **How do you think they felt about having a son?**

OPTIONAL TAKE ONE EXTRA *If you're married, you might want to bring in a tape of your wedding and show a short, dramatic clip of your ceremony. If you're not married, you probably could borrow a friend's tape. When you watch the clip discuss the changes that were involved for your life (or your friend's life) from that moment on. How did the wedding completely change your identity?*

Point out how the story had come full-circle—from mourning and grief, to exuberant gladness. Naomi, who came back to Israel empty, was now full. The Lord had come through. And Ruth, who was once the lowest of all in socioeconomic status had been redeemed and was now a mother. She was once an outsider, and now she had received high status by marrying a wealthy landowner. (See Optional Extra.)

Have someone read Ruth 4:17b. Point out the honor that it was for Ruth to be chosen to be the great-grandmother of Israel's greatest king. Say: **God certainly does include all of us into his family, no matter what!**

In the following situations, ask students to conjecture what might have happened if Ruth had settled for less than a No Return decision in any of the areas below:

- **What if Ruth had decided to turn around and go back to Moab instead of following her mother-in-law to Israel?**
- **What if Ruth had given up on Naomi and trashed the friendship when things got tough?**
- **What if Ruth had been lazy and said, "Who, me glean? Skip that!"?**
- **What if Ruth had pursued some younger, hotter men to marry instead of patiently waiting for God's plan for her life?**

Hand out pens and paper and have students write down one area in which they are facing a tough decision, one that involves their faith being tested. Have them write the name of this decision on the top of their paper. For example, "How should I handle the fact that my boyfriend dumped me?" Tell them to divide the rest of the paper into three parts. In the first section, have them write out what a "lazy" decision would look like. In our example, a lazy decision might be something like, "Get even with him by spreading vicious rumors about him." Beneath that, have them write the potential "opportunity costs" of such a decision. For example, opportunity cost here might include losing the chance to ever rebuild a friendship or missing out on good, healthy things going on in life because you spend all your time being bitter. Then, in the second section have them write out what a mediocre decision might be, and what the opportunity costs of such a decision might be. Finally, in the third section have them write out what they think a No Return decision might be and what the costs and rewards of that decision would be.

step 4 NEW AND IMPROVED LABELS

Students work on "labels" for themselves and for Ruth.

Hand out blank sheets of paper and have students design labels for Ruth as creatively as possible. First, they should pick a negative label that some people might have been calling her in the beginning of the story; for example, "HELPLESS WIDOW" or "MOABITE LOSER." Then have students design their page to look like a soup can label or other product outer covering. They can write or draw such things as ingredients, slogans, company mascots, or whatever else they think of. (Or see Optional Extra.)

Then, in the same way, have students design labels based on some labels they might have heard used towards them. They should try to paint a label that depicts "how the world might see them." Encourage students share their labels with each other.

Point out that Ruth was labeled. But because she was redeemed by Boaz, she was given an entirely new identity.

In small groups, have students design new labels for Ruth and what her character is at the end of the story, following a "redeemed" theme.
Say: **Just as Boaz redeemed Ruth and bought her back at a high cost, you also have been bought back at a high cost by Jesus Christ, our Redeemer. Just as Ruth's identity before she was redeemed by Boaz was wrapped up in her condition as a helpless, hopeless widow, we had a hopeless, helpless identity before we were redeemed by our Lord. But He has completely and radically changed who we are. He has given us value. He has bought for us a completely new way of life.**

Then have students work individually on new labels for themselves, incorporating the fact that they, too, have been redeemed.

Discuss:
- **How should this affect the way that I live?**
- **What difference should this make in my everyday life?**
- **If I really believed it, what would change about my lifestyle?**

Have students write their own genealogies, including brief descriptions of the godly traits and ungodly flaws that they know about each of their ancestors. Compare this with the family tree of Jesus, which also has some shady characters in it. Point out that Ruth herself had a pretty shady family tree, but was quite blessed and honored by God by being allowed to be included. Students should see the obvious application: God can still take any life that is devoted to Him and make big things out of it, no matter how messed up the family around it is.

Encourage students to think through the applications of having a redeemed identity. Challenge them to "claim their reward," whether that means dreaming big dreams for their lives because they know God can accomplish much, being able to treat others with respect and love because they have first been loved and respected, or walking through life with more self-esteem and higher confidence. (See Optional Extra.)

step 5 HERO IN THE MAKING PARTY

Throw a party celebrating your students' new and improved identities.
In closing, throw a hero party, celebrating the fact that God Embraces Nobodies and Empowers them to be Somebodies. In addition to playing music, eating food that you bring in, and having an upbeat time of toasting grape juice to each other and patting one another on the back, try the following:

Celebrate each student by handing out Hero-In-The-Making Awards. Before making copies of Resource 8, "Hero in the Making Awards," you may want to cut carefully around the border so that you're not copying extraneous stuff. Either have students pair up and fill out the awards for each other, or ahead of time prepare an award for each student yourself. The award should be filled out with a detailed vision of what the award recipient is—or has the potential to become—for God.

One of the ways Ruth was a "heroine" was being a role model to many for some 3,000 years, thanks to the fact that her story was recorded in the Bible. Another way God used her as a heroine was to make her the great grandmother of David, the future king of the land. (See Biblical Fast Forward.)

Obed did carry on the name of Elimelech in Israel's history, but he also carried on the name of Boaz and Ruth. He was the grandfather of eight grandsons, the youngest of which was David, the most famous king of Israel and a man after God's own heart, from whose lineage would come Jesus, the Messiah.

Thank God for each one of your students and pray for the ways that He might transform them and use them as heroes. Finally, thank God for being the Redeemer through Jesus Who bought us a completely new future.

THIS CERTIFIES THAT

_____

IS OFFICIALLY A

Because this person has been redeemed by Jesus Christ,
the potential to be a hero is great. Some of the outstanding,
heroic characteristics of this person that I see include:

_____

_____

_____

_____

_____

_____

_____   _____
Signature   Date